A CHRISTMAS
to Remember

FOREWORD

The carols in this collection are composed to help capture the unique spirit, wonder and excitement of the Christmas season.

While maintaining a good balance between melody and accompaniment, feel free to experiment with generous amounts of pedal and other creative interpretations.

I hope the playing of these compositions will help make this a Christmas to remember and cherish.

Merry Christmas,

Randall Hartsell

CONTENTS

Alfred

Amaryllis Painting: Amaryllis (Hippeastrum).
P. J. Redoute. 1827-1833.
The Granger Collection, New York.
Art Direction: Ted Engelbart
Cover Design: Jane Wong

Deck the Halls

Welsh Carol
arr. Randall Hartsell

Moderately and tranquilly

Angels We Have Heard on High

Traditional French Carol
arr. Randall Hartsell

O Little Town of Bethlehem

Lewis H. Redner
arr. Randall Hartsell

*The D natural in the melody is intentional.

Bring a Torch, Jeanette Isabella

Traditional
arr. Randall Hartsell

In the Bleak Midwinter

Gustav Holst
arr. Randall Hartsell

Jingle Bells

James Pierpont
arr. Randall Hartsell

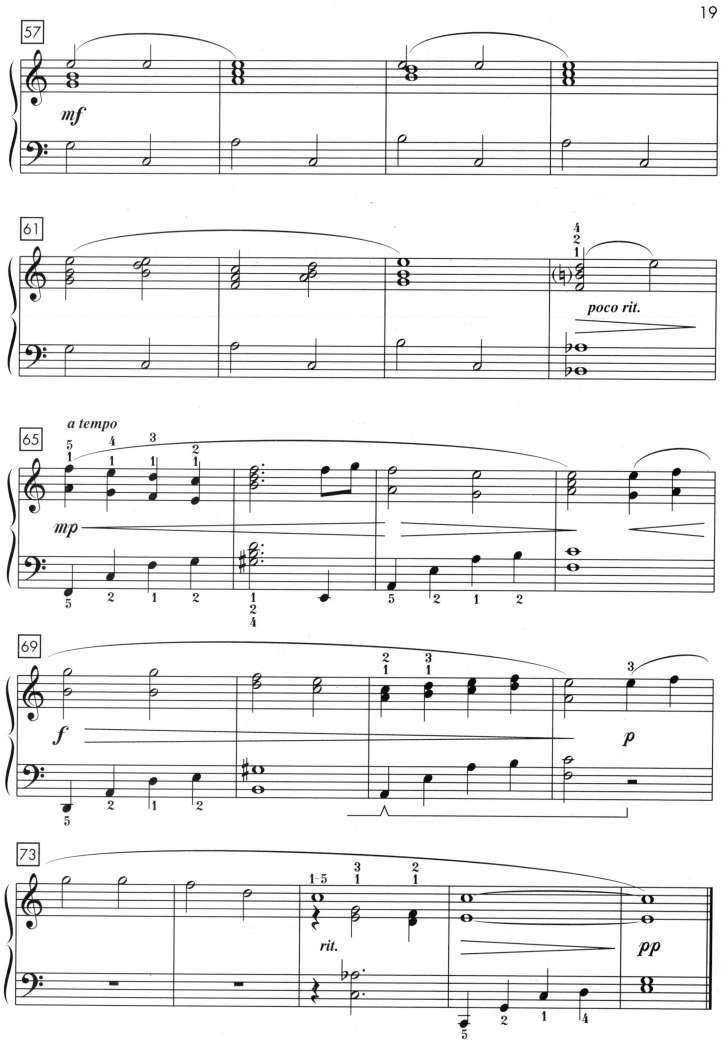

Carol of the Bells

M. Leontovich
arr. Randall Hartsell

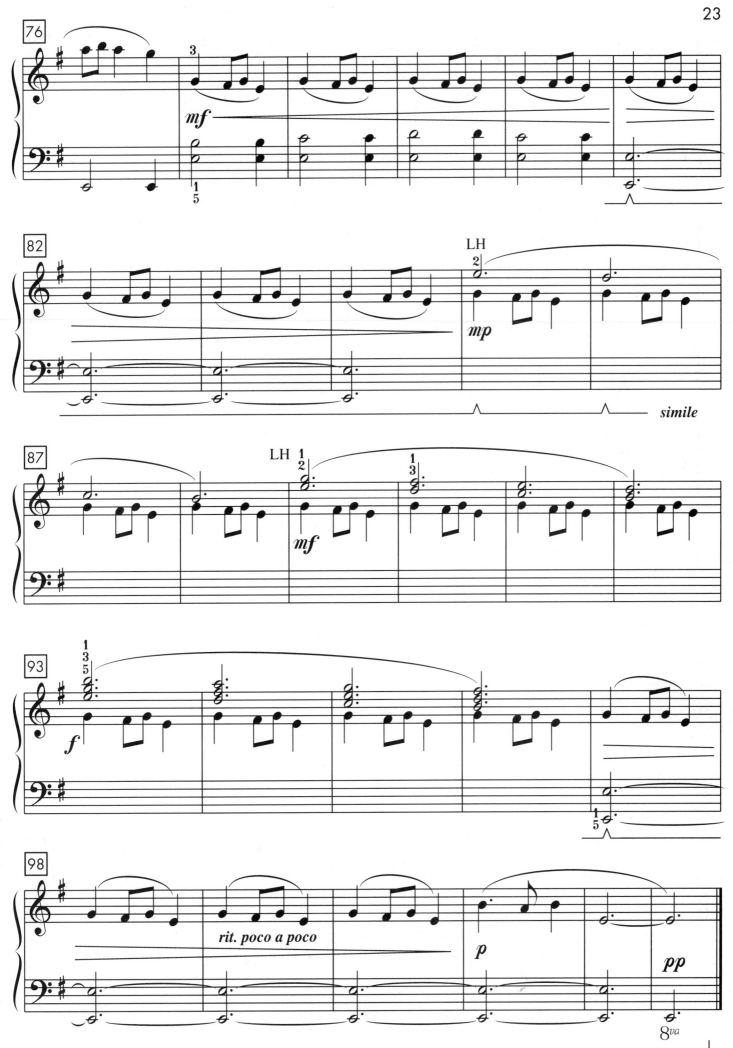

God Rest Ye Merry, Gentlemen

Traditional
arr. Randall Hartsell

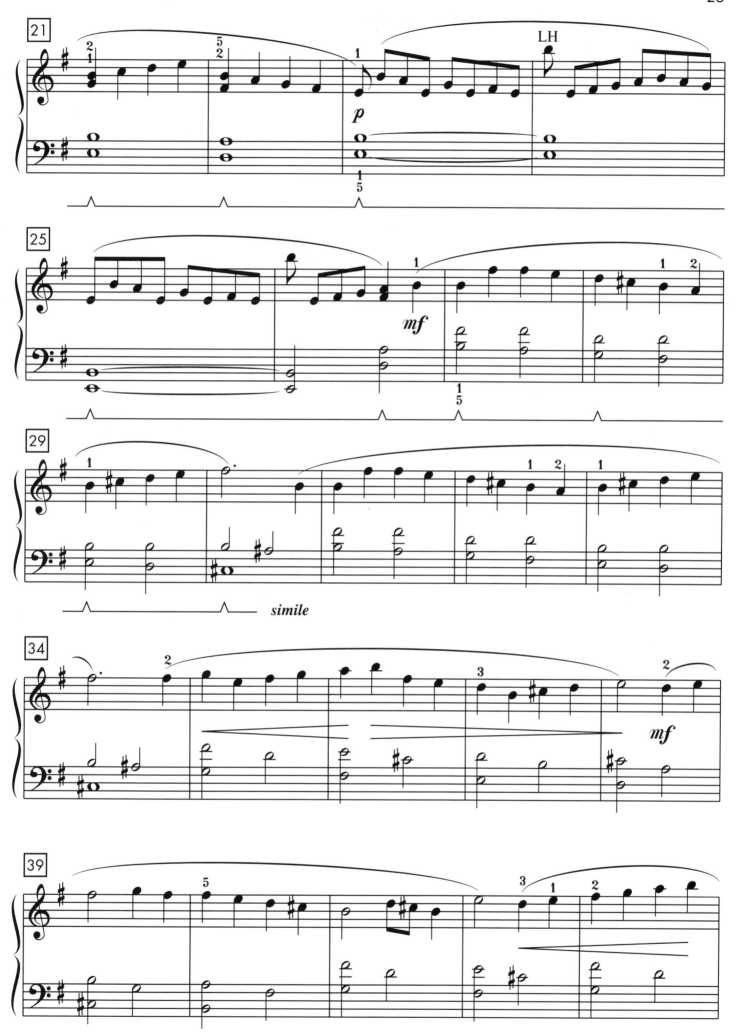

26

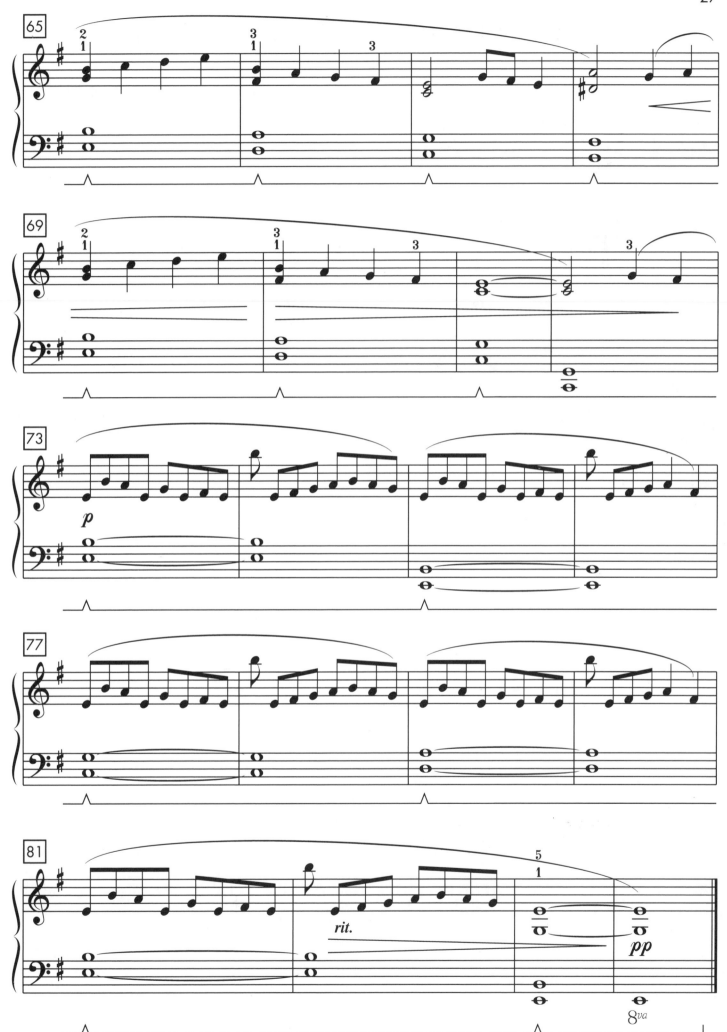

A Christmas to Remember

Moderato

Randall Hartsell

far be - yond this Christ - mas time.

Let this Christ - mas be re - mem - bered the most be -

cause we lis - tened to our hearts and

minds. *mp* *p*

mp Could this be a Christ - mas to re - mem - ber?